Robert Quackenbush

AHOY! AHOY! ARE YOU THERE?

A STORY OF ALEXANDER GRAHAM BELL

Prentice-Hall, Inc.

ENGLEWOOD CLIFFS, NEW JERSEY

Printed in the United States of America   ·J

Prentice-Hall International, Inc., London
Prentice-Hall of Australia, Pty. Ltd., North Sydney
Prentice-Hall of Canada, Ltd., Toronto
Prentice-Hall of India Private Ltd., New Delhi
Prentice-Hall of Japan, Inc., Tokyo
Prentice-Hall of Southeast Asia Pte. Ltd., Singapore
Whitehall Books Limited, Wellington, New Zealand

10 9 8 7 6 5 4 3 2 1

Library of Congress Cataloging in Publication Data

Quackenbush, Robert M.
    Ahoy! Ahoy! Are you there?

    SUMMARY: A humorous account of events in the life
of the inventor of the telephone.
    1. Bell, Alexander Graham, 1847-1922—Juvenile
literature. 2. Inventors—United States—Biography.
[1. Bell, Alexander Graham, 1847-1922. 2. Inventors]
I. Title.
TK6143.B4Q3   621.385'092'4 [B] [92]   81-7386
ISBN 0-13-020776-4   AACR2

From a very early age, Alexander Bell had an inventive and inquisitive mind. Born in Edinburgh, Scotland, in 1847, he was the son and grandson of well-known speech teachers. At one time his grandfather had been an actor. So it was no wonder that the young Bell had a flair for the dramatic as well as a streak of whimsy. Having no middle name, he decided to give himself one when he was eleven. He chose the name of a Canadian friend. "Call me Graham," he told everyone. Then he probably set out on one of his many investigations, such as watching a cat jump off a porch to see why it landed on all four paws.

9

Graham was also a talented pianist. Many people believed he was headed for the concert stage. But Graham was more interested in his father's work. Alexander Melville Bell was the inventor of something called Visible Speech, that showed how sounds are made in people's mouths. The sounds were translated into pictures and symbols to show how words could be spoken in any language. Graham became so good at understanding his father's charts that he would ask his friends to test him. One time when he left the room where the test was being given, a trick was played on him. But when Graham came back, he said every sound that his friends had asked his father to write down in symbols. Together the sounds made a yawn!

When Graham finished school, he began studying the human ear and working on speech experiments of his own. He made use of every ear and voice box around him—even his pet terrier's. He figured out how to press the dog's mouth and vocal cords so that its growls sounded like human words. "How are you, Grandmother?" the dog would say. Graham also created a device shaped like a human skull that had a mouth, tongue, larynx, and bellows; these produced a voice that cried "MAMA!" The loud wail of this strange contraption often brought a neighbor running to see what was the matter. Graham was on to something, but no one knew what it was at this point, not even Graham himself.

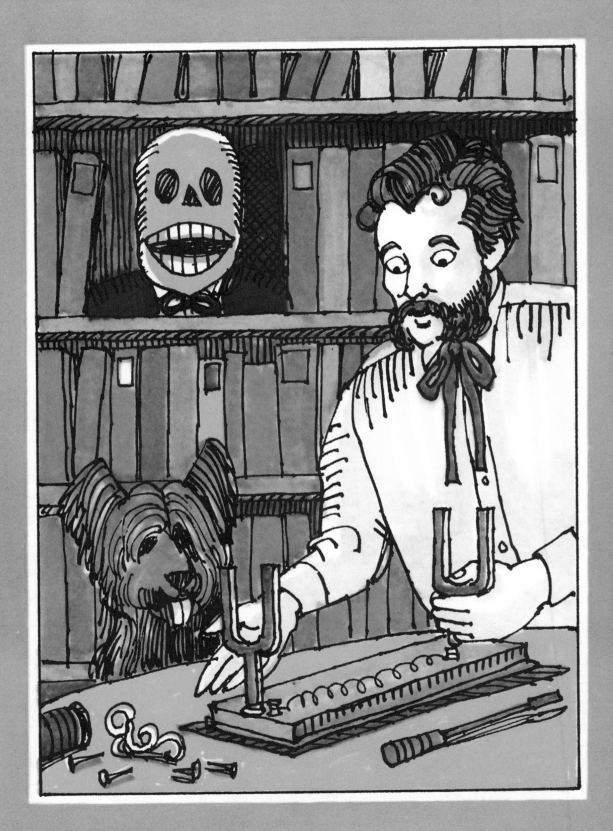

Then Graham turned to experimenting with tuning forks. He was impressed with the discoveries of the great German scientist Hermann Ludwig von Helmholtz, who had been able to reproduce vowel sounds by vibrating tuning forks electrically. Graham discovered for himself that when a fork of a certain tone, or pitch, vibrates, another fork of the same pitch also vibrates. At last Graham knew where he was headed. He wanted to invent a new kind of telegraph that could send many messages over the same wire—each message being sent at a different pitch that could be received by a receiver of the same pitch. This would be called a "harmonic telegraph." More than that, he hoped to invent a machine that could send the human voice by wire.

15

When Graham was twenty-four, the Bell family moved to Ontario, Canada. Graham himself went to Boston to teach at the Boston School for the Deaf, using his father's Visible Speech methods. He was immediately successful as a teacher. He was also in demand for private tutoring. One private pupil was a pretty seventeen-year-old girl named Mabel Hubbard. Mabel had been totally deaf since she was five years old and as a result she had lost much of her ability to talk. Another private pupil was a little boy named Georgie Sanders who had been born deaf. Graham's hours were nearly filled with his teaching, but he still found time at night to work on his "harmonic telegraph" and his "talking machine." Staying up late didn't bother him because he didn't need much sleep. He called himself a "night owl."

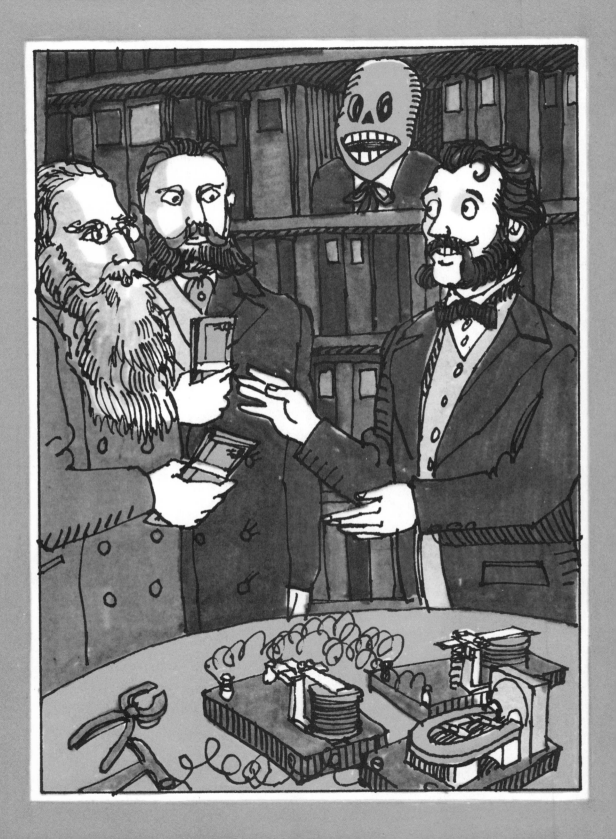

Both Mabel's father, Gardiner Hubbard, and Georgie's father, Thomas Sanders, became interested in Graham's "harmonic telegraph." Being wealthy men, they offered Graham money to support his experiments. Graham gladly took a leave from teaching so that he could devote full time to his inventions. He hired an assistant, Thomas A. Watson, and the two set to work, first in an electrical shop and then in their boarding house. They were able to draw up patentable plans for a "harmonic telegraph," but they could not perfect a working model. They realized that they were a long way from doing that. And so, unknown to Hubbard and Sanders, they put most of their energies into developing Graham's "talking machine"—which he now called the telephone.

19

All sounds, including human speech, are vibrations that travel through the air or other substances in varying patterns called sound waves. To send a sound by wire, Graham knew he had to find a way to turn sound waves into electrical signals that could be carried by wire. The continuous electric current had to grow stronger and weaker, just as the vibrations that formed the sounds did. Graham was sure that this could be done. He plunged into a maze of wires, electromagnets, and batteries.

One of Graham's experimental telegraph models became a clue to the perfection of the telephone. It had tiny metal reeds in place of tuning forks. And Graham discovered by accident that when the model's sending, or transmitting, reed was flicked with a finger, it transmitted a vibrating, or undulating, electric current. The undulating current traveled through a connecting wire to the model's receiver and set the receiver reed vibrating in tune with the first reed. The electrical signals were reproducing the sound wave made by the reed. With this discovery, Graham knew that the invention of the telephone was close at hand. But unknown to him, a race was on. Out in Ohio, a man named Elisha Gray was also well on his way toward inventing the telephone. Then trouble came. Hubbard found out what Graham was doing and insisted that he go back to making a model for the "harmonic telegraph." About the same time, Watson got sick. And as if that weren't enough, Graham fell in love with Mabel but she wasn't interested in him. Discouraged, Graham gave up everything and went back to teaching.

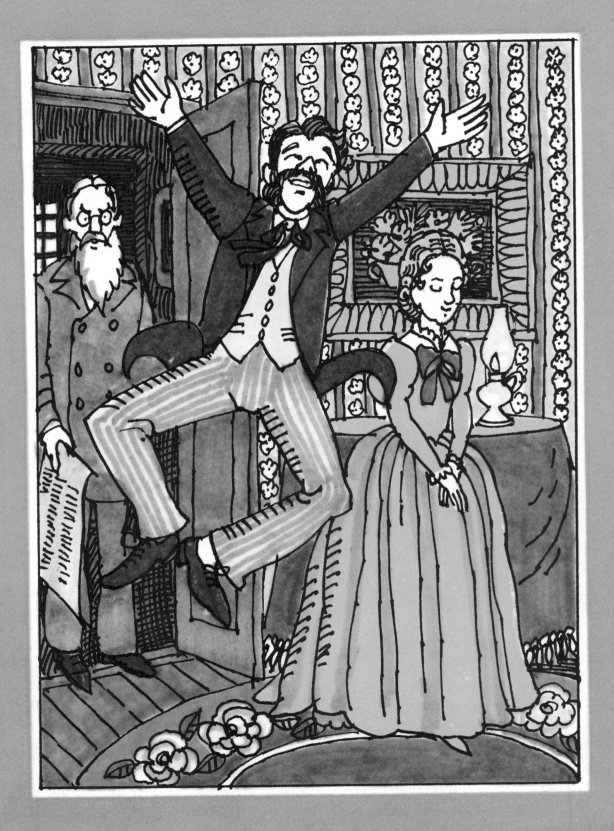

Hubbard was furious. He insisted that Graham get back to work on his inventions—and that now included the telephone. But Graham refused. The two argued for months. In the end, it was Mabel who solved the problem. Suddenly, she changed her mind about Graham. On her eighteenth birthday, she told him that, except for her mother, she loved him more than anyone in the world. They became engaged at once. So everything ended happily. Graham rushed to draw up his plans for the telephone. Hubbard took the plans to Washington, D.C., so that the rights to the invention would be protected. And just in time, too! A few hours after Graham's papers were received, Elisha Gray arrived at the patent offices. He was too late. Graham had already won the race!

Patent or not, the telephone still did not speak. It mumbled and muttered. Graham and Watson got busy. They created a speaking-tube mouthpiece and a reed receiver, each with its own battery and electromagnet. The mouthpiece had a round paper-thin piece of metal at the bottom. Behind this was a needle that controlled the flow of the electrical current. The needle dipped down into a dish filled with water plus a little sulfuric acid. The idea was that the thin metal would vibrate as voice sounds reached it. Its vibrations would push the needle, making it rise and fall in the acid, and this would strengthen and weaken the electrical current in the wire, making it an undulating current. The undulating current would travel through a long wire to the reed receiver, which would convert the electrical signals back into sounds. On March 10, 1876, the model was finished. And the first telephone message was spoken by Graham. "Mr. Watson—come here—I want you," was the historic call.

His music, his talking machines, his study of Visible Speech, and finally his experiments with electricity—all together led Graham to his final triumph. In May 1876, he demonstrated the first practical telephone before a committee of the world's leading scientists in Philadelphia. His invention created a sensation. By 1877, Graham, with Hubbard and Sanders, had founded the Bell Telephone Company to develop the telephone business. That summer Graham and Mabel were married. The happy couple went to England on their honeymoon. There Graham was invited to demonstrate his telephone to Queen Victoria. The queen was very impressed—so much so that she didn't seem to mind when Graham, in his excitement, touched her arm to get her attention. But the rest of the court gasped in horror at his lack of respect.

The early days of the telephone were not without problems. To Graham's disappointment, the standard answer changed from his jolly "Ahoy!" to the commonplace "Hello." The first operators were men who didn't have very good telephone manners. They cursed and used such coarse language that they had to be replaced with women who wouldn't offend customers. Even bigger problems would pop up as the demand for telephones increased. By 1888, for example, there were almost 200,000 telephones in the United States. In large cities, the skies were nearly blackened by all the overhead wires that were needed. It was only in New York's great blizzard of '88, when lines were pulled down by the storm, that people realized how unsafe they were. By 1900 they were all placed underground and city skies were cleared.

In 1881, Graham decided he wanted to work independently. He left the Bell Telephone Company and established his own laboratories. One was the Volta Laboratory in Washington, D.C., where wax cylinders and discs for phonograph recording were invented, launching the record industry. With his share of the profits, Graham established the Volta Bureau, which still carries on the study of deafness. For the next forty-one years of his life, he had the pleasure of doing whatever he wanted. He relaxed and slept till noon on his estate in Nova Scotia. But he never stopped experimenting, and there were no limits to his imagination. He would raid the kitchen and "borrow" Mabel's dishpans to make a set of floating wheels for a model hydrofoil. Or several Venetian blinds would "disappear" from the porch windows, only to turn up later in a model propeller. He built and tested magnificent kites on his front lawn. Whatever Graham did, you may be sure he was enjoying life to the fullest.

Epilogue

In 1875, when Alexander Graham Bell learned how to make current undulate over wire and invented a machine that translated sound into electrical signals, he discovered a new way for human beings to communicate. His invention of the telephone made the world smaller. But Bell's magnificent achievements went beyond the invention of the telephone and his discovery of the basic principles of the multiple telegraph. Throughout his life he continued to devote himself to new experiments. His numerous other inventions included the photophone that could send speech by light waves, an early iron lung, the hydrofoil speedboat, and ailerons for airplane wings, to keep the plane steady in flight. He also founded many organizations, including the Aerial Experiment Association. Even so, with all that Bell did, his greatest achievement was as a celebrated teacher of the deaf. He had reached thousands of deaf-mute children (among them Helen Keller) and had shown them the way to speech. And this, he said, was how he would prefer to be remembered.

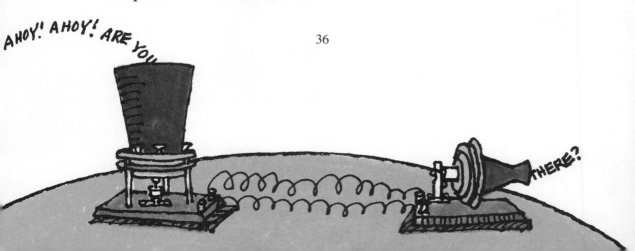